MY GLIMPSE INTO GOD'S PARADISE

Jim O'Neal

ISBN 979-8-89112-794-4 (Paperback)
ISBN 979-8-89112-795-1 (Digital)

Covenant Books
11661 Hwy 707
Murrells Inlet, SC 29576
www.covenantbooks.com

ACKNOWLEDGMENTS

I want to thank my brother, Rick O'Neal, for his support and help with making this all happen.

I want to thank Jeri Burger for her fantastic artwork. Her vision of my dream is like she was there with me.

I want to thank my sister, Patsy Shields, and my granddaughter, Madysen O'Neal, for their encouragement and support to go ahead and put my dream in writing.

And I want to thank Lowell Shields for the photographs he furnished.

My dream begins as quickly as it ends.

As I opened my eyes, I was in a world that I had never seen before, it was a world that you only dream of seeing. I just stood there for a while, trying to figure out where I was and how I got here. I had never seen or been to this place before, but there was a sense of happiness, peace, and love.

I was leaning next to a red brick column, with a warm sun and a gentle breeze, welcoming me to this strange place. I could hear songbirds in the distance and the chatter of hundreds of people talking.

It still was not clear to me what was happening or what had happened or why I was here. I started looking around for something that would give me a clue as to where I was and why. There was nothing here that looked familiar. So it was time to look around for clues, something to tell me why I was at this beautiful place.

There wasn't just one column, like the one I was standing by, but hundreds of them, spaced about sixteen feet apart with beautiful arches between each one of them. These columns and arches continued for as far as the eye could see, and all these columns supported a beautiful red-brick building.

I was looking to the south, and adjacent to this building was a very beautiful wooden boardwalk made from the finest hardwood lumber. This boardwalk was attached to this brick building and extended out from the building. And it, too, continued as far as the eye could see. This boardwalk reached out about one hundred yards to the west.

Each column was one of thousands that were holding an open-faced building that was facing to the west. I turned around and saw that this magnificent construction went to the north as far as the eye could see.

Later in this dream, the significance of this magnificent building, being the same from one end to the other, was explained to me. No matter what kind of life you lived on earth, you enter God's kingdom the same way. God judges everyone with the same set of laws. The evil and wicked, murderers, and sinners all enter into God's kingdom the same way as the followers of God (the souls that have followed in the ways of the Lord). It is in God's kingdom, where He lays out His judgment on these lost souls. Everyone is judged equally. We all enter God's kingdom the same way.

When I first opened my eyes, I was wearing a suit; I assumed that I had died. Yes, it was very clear to me that I had died, but there were so many questions to be answered. Now I saw myself in everyday clothing.

As I stood there watching, there were hundreds of people walking up and down the boardwalk. Some were sitting on benches and chairs; some were admiring the many potted flowers and plants that were abundantly placed up and down this boardwalk. Everyone was enjoying this beautiful day, smiling and chatting with each other.

Looking to the west, the sun was about at two o'clock stage, making for a perfect day, but it also furnished this magnificent building with its only light source. Warm sunrays were shining between each archway, reaching deep into this very large building.

At the edge of this boardwalk, there was a railing with openings every so often, allowing for a passage going out to a lush green field. This field is loaded with beautiful flowers of every variety and color and thousands of birds of every different color and size, with each having their own song that fills your heart with joy. In the distance, there was a large variety of beautiful green trees of all different shapes and sizes.

There were people setting in conversation, while dogs, horses, and all kinds of creatures supplied entertainment for all. The sky was a beautiful blue, with soft white clouds floating carelessly and a gentle breeze that almost took your breath away. This was a masterpiece that only a master artist could create.

People were walking by me, smiling and asking how I was doing and with true concern. This gave me a sense of belonging here and maybe the courage to go check this place out. I stood up straight and walked to the closest opening to the building. Looking inside this building, it was very dark. The only light was from the two o'clock sun, shining through the opening. There were hundreds of people inside. Like outside, they were enjoying time with each other. And there too was the array of colorful flowers, soaking up the sun.

There was a large crowd of people standing around what looked like a large water fountain that was not working. Their faces were filled with hope and great anticipation. For what? I did not know. I was totally puzzled as to what was going on. Suddenly, water went ten feet in the air. Even for me, it was a magnificent sight. The crowd cheered like it was something spectacular. I still did not know the significance of it all. There had to be a greater meaning to this. (I would learn later.)

While I was watching, I saw my sister, Patsy, on the other side of the crowd. (I was seeing her in her younger years, with a large smile and a face full of happiness and peace.) I went to greet her. She met me with a smile but wasn't really surprised to see me. She already knew I was coming. We talked a while, and in our conversation, I asked why everyone was so excited about the water fountain. She explained to me why the water was such an important event.

Like many times in my dream, she had something she had to go do but said she would catch up with me later. Later in my dream, this too would become clear to me as to why she always had something to do.

And like in life, she always said, "I love you."

The water and the wood boardwalk and red bricks would come to have a greater meaning later in my dream.

As I walked back outside, I noticed the air was pure and untarnished. This was a reminder of how we have abused and tarnished our world. We have filled our air with chemicals, smoke, and foul odors. All these are the by-products of things that we never needed. In the beginning, God gave us everything we needed in the purest form, and we disregarded His goodness, and we wanted more for our own pleasures and greed.

I reclaimed my original spot by the red brick column, where I stood for what seemed like hours. I was trying to take in where this magnificent place could be, not knowing how. But it was becoming clear to me where I was. It was like I was being fed the knowledge of what had happened, and in this knowledge, I also learned that time has no priorities here.

When I speak of time, it is only in a human's way of thinking.

As I was standing there, taking this all in, I heard a voice that only a father would recognize. I was looking hard for where this voice was coming from. In my search for this voice that I knew was my son, I saw a group of young men laughing and having a good time. I located the voice; it was coming from a young, goodlooking man. It was my son, but he too was in his younger years, strong and full of life. At the same time, he spotted me. It was like he knew that someone was looking for him. He got up and left the group of young men to meet with me. We hug for a long time. This was a joy that I had missed for a long time but at the same time a great sadness. I had not known that he had passed before me.

This would be my main and greatest hesitation to write about this dream.

Just like my sister, he was glad to see me but not very surprised. We had not seen each other for a long while and had a lot to discuss and memories to relive. He told me that he knew that I was coming and was waiting to see me.

Before we parted and said "I will see you later," he told me that this was a place of learning. "We are all students and teachers at the same time. You will learn from others, and they will learn from you. There are so many questions to be answered. You will learn God's answer to all questions.

"This is our God's home. In God's home, there is not hunger or thirst, and evil has no access to His kingdom. Everyone you see here, you see them as you would remember them on earth. You are seeing their soul, not their worldly body. The people you don't know, you will see them not as a stranger but as a friend. You will only see the good in them, for we are not to judge anyone. At this point God has already judged each of us. Everyone's rewards or punishment, whichever it may be, is here in God's home and for everyone to see.

"At this place, there is no hunger or thirst, so there are no meals. There is no nighttime. God has brought us out of the darkness into the light. There is no such thing as time here or the need for a schedule. Here you learn that the body and soul are two different things. The body needs to eat and drink. The body needs to sleep, therefore there was darkness, which gives the body time to rest. Schedules and time are only needed to support the body. Even the Son of God ate and drank while he was here on earth. Your soul needs none of these things.

"In God's home, there is a north, south, east, and west. These facts are only in God's house.

"North is closer to God. So if you were very close to Him in your life, then you are placed close to Him in His kingdom, which is further to the north. If you lived a wicked and evil life, then you are placed further to the south but still in His kingdom. East is where you come from or the beginning. The east is always your past. Do not look backward. (Your past is full of sins and wrongdoings.) The past is done. You cannot change it. Always look to the future to improve on your past. Only use your past to improve on your future. The west is the future. The reason we are facing the west is because the west is always the future. On earth, the sun comes up in the east, that is the beginning of each day, and you end your day when the sun sets in the west.

"On earth, you were offered a new beginning each day. Each new day, you are given a new chance to improve your life. If you truly ask for forgiveness, all of yesterday's sins are already forgiven. This is because Jesus died on the cross to cover for every one's sins. Therefore, everyone is offered a new beginning each day.

"The word truly is a very important word. There is a big difference between asking forgiveness and truly being sorry for your bad doings. You must be *truly* sorry for your wrongdoings.

"Here in God's kingdom, He offers you a next life in hopes you will live it in the ways of the Lord.

"If you were an evil person in your former life, then you will be reborn into an evil beginning. (This is what we would consider as going to hell.) It will be your choice, in your next life, to live a godly life. Even in this new life, God allows you to take some of your knowledge that you have gained from this place and your former life into your next. God truly wants everyone to succeed."

While I was taking in the beauty of this place, my sister, Pasty, came and sat down with me. She would be one of my many teachers. She handed me a device that resembled a large combination padlock. (I will call it my locket of memories or inventory of life.) She explained that it was a total inventory of my entire life on earth. Only God and I could open it. I could open it at any time, and it was mine to keep. God wanted me to see every minute of every day of my life and to learn from it. It showed me everything I ever said or done, good and bad. It showed me all the good things I had done and how it impacted other people's lives. But most of all, it showed me all the bad, evil, and selfish things I had done and the feelings I hurt and the damage I caused in other people's lives.

By the time I finished viewing my life, I was so ashamed of myself. I had done more evil than good. I was a selfish man. I cheated, lied, and used other people for my own gain. I had made many promises and failed to keep most of them, leaving other people to pay for my wrongdoings. There were many occasions that I could have spoken up for God, defended Him in a conversation, or even confessed that I believed in God. It was easier to keep quiet so I could fit in with the crowd. Knowing God and denying that you believe in Him is not looked upon very lightly. If you believe in God, let the whole world know it and be very proud that you know Him.

It was hard to believe that God had forgiven me for all the bad I had done. But when you are truly sorry, and God has forgiven you, the past is the past.

It showed me when God was by my side when I needed Him. He was always there when I needed Him in my dark days. He answered every prayer in one way or another (sometimes the answer was no, but it would be for my good), and He comforted me through my sad times.

Sometimes the answer *no* means that he has a better plan for you.

While in this place, you are encouraged to walk and see the punishments or rewards for doing or not doing God's will. I don't have a name for this place, so I will call it God's kingdom.

I was taught when God created the earth. He made everything very simple. He made man and a woman and made a thing we call love. He made us have feelings. He introduced kindness and giving. He made nothing complicated, just a man and a woman. He gave them all the food and drink they needed. He taught them to love each other and be good to each other. He taught them that they were not the same, that they had different roles in life, and not to compete against each other. He taught them to build shelters and make food and to have a family. All very simple and good, and all they needed to do was to believe in Him. But through time, man complicated everything. Man introduced lust, greed, lies, cheat, murder, and deception.

The north, south, east, and west that I speak of in this next paragraph are not the same as the directions that are in God's kingdom.

God created the earth and the sun. Along with this, He created the north and south and east and west. The sun would rise in the east and set in the west. By watching the sun as it traveled through the sky, you could tell what time of day it was. Instead of a watch, this was God's way of telling the time of day. North and south, by watching the sun as it traveled from north to south and south to north, was God's way of telling us the time of year it was. This way of telling time was very accurate and true and has never changed since the beginning of time.

The moon was not mentioned in my dream, but it, too, is a very important and consistent timekeeper. The moon orbits the earth thirteen times a year (every twenty-seven days, seven hours, and forty-three minutes). The moon is not needed in paradise, for there is no nighttime.

But there again, God used His paintbrush to paint us more nighttime masterpieces. Nighttime is for giving the body rest and a time for romance. He gave us the moonlight with shooting stars. He gave us starlight nights and the northern lights with their magnificent array of colors. He gave us the bright moon, shining down on a snow-covered mountain pass, making for a romantic horse-and-buggy ride. (The moon lightens the way and the cold night air, making it very appropriate to hold each other close to stay warm.) Moon and stars were also made for falling in love.

These magnificent nighttime masterpieces are some of his most prized creations—creations he made to warm the hearts of a man and woman that are meant to be together. This is favorably looked upon by God. They are in His plans for a man and a woman to find and fall in love under a starlit night and a full moon that sends His blessings.

Can you imagine a life without a moonlit night, without stars to help guide your way, without the silence of a gentle breeze to ease your troubled mind? (Now that I am an old man, I look back and remember these nights and how much they meant to me.)

Remember that the North Star guided the three wise men to Bethlehem, where Jesus was born.

Advice to the young: Do not let this pass you by. God created this for you. Take the time to enrich your lives. God did not intend for you to be alone.

The artist Jesse Barnes captured many of God's masterpieces in his paintings.

Back to my dream.

Then came a time when I noticed that to the far, far, far southwest, the sky was a little darker, like just before a storm. Wanting to learn more about God's home, I started walking south on the boardwalk to see why. But shortly after I began my walk, a young man started walking with me. We stopped for a while to chat, and he explained that when you look to the west (which God called your future, your new beginning), your right arm will be pointing to the north, and your left arm will be pointing to the south. As you remember, when Jesus ascended into heaven, He sat on the right side of God the Father. Therefore, when you look to the north, the sky will be brighter, and the south will be darker. And you will learn as you walk south what the meaning is. He chatted awhile longer and parted with a smile. This was one of my many lessons (the further north I went, the closer I got to God, and the further south I went was closer to evil). So if God placed your soul far enough south, it would be considered hell but without the devil or evil to torture or harm you. You must remember, God is a loving God, and He created your soul. God has no intention of giving up on a soul that He created.

This journey would answer many questions. And I would make this journey many times while I am here. But I always come back to where God placed me. There's one thing to remember about where God placed me in His kingdom; this boardwalk and magnificent building continued to the north, as far as the eye can see. So this means that I did not live a perfect life on earth. But God judged me with a very kind heart.

As I walked down this boardwalk, which was endless and darker the farther I traveled, the smile on people's faces started to fade. They were feeling shame and regret for the lives they had lived. Their faded smiles turned into tears, and then people sat, crying and holding their heads in sorrow. These people had been evil, wicked, had murdered, and they were people who knew God but had a hatred for Him. So this was where God put them on this boardwalk of life. This was their judgment.

There was so much to learn on this walk. I want to come back again to learn more. One of the biggest sins is to know God but reject Him. And again, even these wicked souls will be given another chance. And again, these lost souls can take some of these lessons into your next life. But their next life will begin in a very bad place, but they will be given every opportunity to gain salvation.

(In my writings, I jump from one subject to another.)

I sat down with my son and sister and asked where my parents were. They had been here but had already moved on to their next life. I asked for them to explain. "If you are asked if you want to go to your next life, you can or you can stay here as long as you want." My parents chose to go to their next life. The process is, you take inventory of your old life, and you go down the steps into the greenfield. You walk until you find a nice place to bury your old life, and it will be buried forever. But the knowledge you have gained from your old life and the teachings of God can be taken with you. You then keep walking west, which is the direction of a new life and a new beginning. There you bury your old life, which will be marked for you so that other loved ones can bury their old lives close to yours.

Many of our conversations would take place in the grassy meadow, in the cool shade of a large white oak tree. On most occasions, we would have the company of other souls, joining in our conversations. None of us had anything to hide. We all enjoyed hearing about each other's journey through life. The best way to learn is to listen, and the best way to teach is to speak and tell your story.

The reason for this place is to be a learning place; it is so you may be able to improve your next life in the eyes of God. So from as far south as you can go to as far north as you can go, you have another chance to improve your next life. No matter how bad things are, God still loves them all. If you had evil parents in your last life, you do not have to be born to either one of them. Your new life can be totally different than from your old life.

On my next journey to this dark place (this place that we would consider hell), I paid more attention to the different types of people that were there. There were fancy suits, thieves, and people who didn't care about anyone but themselves. These people didn't need God when they were on earth. (In the Bible, it says that it is as hard for a rich man to enter the gates of heaven as it is for a camel to pass through the eye of a needle.) A rich man has everything he needs or wants, so he does not need God, but a poor man needs God every day. So all the people that are here on the dark part of the boardwalk are either too rich to need God, or they are just evil people. But still, God is giving them another chance in their next life.

Lesson learned, to be truly a rich man, you do not have to have a lot of money or worldly goods. True wealth is in your heart and soul.

On my next trip, I walked very slowly, trying to take in all that was being taught to me as I left what now I call my homeplace with such beauty. As I was going along, the lush green grass now had some weeds and dead grass, and the trees were now a different species, where there were flowers now were dead bushes. When I got as far as I wanted to go, the bushes were now briar patches, trees were now thorn trees, fields were barren, and the sky was black rolling clouds. Even though this was where God put these people to bury their old lives, He also promised them a new chance, a new life, a new choice for a better life. I don't know why, but I would visit this place many times.

As I journey farther in this direction, the landscape became very harsh and unbearable. At first, I thought that there weren't very many lost souls here, but they were here. They were hiding in the darkest parts of this building. They were hiding partly from the harsh conditions but mostly out of shame. In our way of thinking, they were close to being in hell, or they were in hell. We were taught that hell was darkness and fire and pain and was forever. This was close, but it was not forever. These souls could go to their next life, with God by their side.

I wondered why I continued to make this journey. God created the word (curious, the desire to learn).

I have asked myself why I never went to the north. It was closer to God. These souls had lived a more God-fearing life and was rewarded a more perfect spot in God's kingdom. This question has bothered me for years. The word *curiosity* comes into play. Why wasn't I curious? I could have learned so much from them. Maybe I was ashamed of myself. Maybe I was envious of them. It couldn't be envious because that word does not exist in heaven. It must be that I was ashamed of myself. Come to think of it; the souls that were far to the south or dark side never ventured to my place.

Back where I now call home, I could not find my sister. When I asked where she might be, it was explained to me that she had been called on by God to go to her next life. There was to be a baby born to a young Christian family. This was a couple that loved each other, heart and soul, and loved God even more. And this baby would bring much love and joy to this family. But sadly, this baby would not live very long. This was not to be a punishment from God but a true test of their faith. If they truly trusted in God and believed in His word, they would know that God was caring for this soul, and they would see her again.

This would truly test my faith. This would be very hard to take.

My sister was to be this baby. My sister was called upon to be this gift, this test, for this young couple.

My sister was one of God's chosen souls. I did remember that she always would be called to the north, which was closer to God. This also meant that she would be coming back to her place in God's kingdom soon.

This also explained to me why there were no babies or young children here.

Not having a sense of time here, it wasn't very long before Patsy was back with Stormy and me, having long conversations under our favorite oak tree.

This brought up another question for me—a question that I never asked about and a question I never had an answer for. Pasty was the soul of my sister, the soul of my parent's daughter, and the soul of Storm's aunts. Now she was also the soul of a baby girl that belonged to a loving young couple.

This was too complicated for me, so I will move on.

Back to other lessons learned. Back at the water fountain, people took great joy in seeing the water fountain working. This was a celebration of the holy water, not the fountain itself. Water was and still is the most important and valued substance on the face of the earth. There is no life of any kind that can live without water. But it is the most abused, neglected, and wasted substance on earth. On earth, water can be heated hot enough to kill germs and help with healing and to cook our food. Water can be frozen solid or made into vaper. Water is used for travel, up and down rivers and across the oceans. You drink it, and you wash in it. Water was also used for baptism, the giver of life and a spiritual rebirth. (You cannot do any of these things with diamonds, silver, or gold.)

Baptism is an acknowledgment of your faith in God.

The boardwalk was made of the finest lumber to be seen. This brings us to the trees. God gave us trees. Trees are a food source; they bear fruit and nuts. They cool us with their shade and can keep us warm with their fire. We build our shelters to keep us safe from the weather. And most of all, they give us oxygen to breathe. They also stand for beauty and strength. They provide a home for wildlife and birds. Some are giant flowering trees with a large array of colors, colors that add to the beauty of this paradise. Trees are renewable, if one is cut down or dies, another one takes its place. All it takes is one seed, water, and mother earth. This has been going on for thousands of years.

And the red bricks were made from the earth, water, and the warming rays of the sun. This too helps keep us safe and warm. All these things are put here by our Creator.

(When we think about it, the body we leave behind when we pass is made 100 percent from Mother Earth.) Our bodies are made from some of the same elements as red bricks. (The human body is also a renewable source.)

This is another one of God's perfect creations. Water is made partly of oxygen, which comes from trees. Trees need water and earth to grow. The earth needs water so it can give rebirth to the trees and plants. All this is to sustain life as we know it on earth.

Another thing in my dream was, I asked if I had any other siblings pass through here. Did they meet with God's favor? The answer was yes, one of my older sisters. She stayed here for some time. She had already moved on before Stormy arrived. But she and Patsy had spent a lot of time together. They too had many long conversations under those beautiful oak trees.

My parents had remarried in their new life, and my older sister went to join them. So that was a big joy for me. This is a testament to the kind of parents we had.

I remember my parents; they were the best parents anyone could ask for. They showed their love for each other and their love for all of us kids. They taught us about God and took us to church. They taught us how to accept that word *no* as an answer. (The word *no* is a very and maybe the most important word when raising a child.) They gave us everything they could and sometimes went without for themselves. God truly blessed us with these two parents.

So many times, in life, God has put two bodies and two souls together that are a perfect match. Their love for each other never dies. When one dies, the remaining one will stay faithful until they too have passed. Their souls can reunite at this place that God has provided.

Remember, when God created Adam and Eve, His intentions was for them to be together forever. God took a rib from Adam to create Eve. Therefore, Eve would always be a part of Adam's life.

Just a reminder, this was not part of my dream. Some of my writings are of my thoughts as I am remembering my dream.

On one occasion, my son and I took a long walk out in the grassy meadow. There was a gentle breeze with blue birds flying from tree to tree. Butterflies were aggravating some small pups that were playing in the tall flowers that were growing around a beautiful lake. The lake had crystal blue water with blooming lily pads that painted a picture that would take your breath away. The sky was a beautiful blue that reminded me of my beautiful granddaughter's blue eyes.

We talked about our former lives, the good times and the sad times. We talked about the possibilities of our next life. In my life on earth, I had two very loving parents. They loved each other. They loved each one of us, and they loved their God. They raised us to live a good life and to follow God's laws. I told my son that I hoped I could have the same parents and siblings.

Stormy's mother and I had been divorced for some time. He and I were not as close as I would have hoped, but I loved him just the same. I told him that I hoped I would have him in my next life. I did not get an answer or a reply; that decision hurt deeply. I had not raised him with the same love and attention that my parents gave me.

At this point, I realized that your soul could feel pain and feel the joy of love and kindness.

Something I want to add at this point: Each time I walked into the meadow, no matter who I was with or if I was alone, there was a total feeling of peace and happiness. In this kingdom, there are no differences in opinions, nothing to argue about. Everything in your heart was good and without evil.

This would give you a feeling that you would want to stay here forever. And again, God welcomes you to stay here as long as you want and even stay here forever. At this time, my thoughts were to stay here forever. Why would I leave? But later I would realize that even your soul longs to be held and loved by another soul.

These are my own thoughts about staying here or going to your next life. If God was in favor of the way, you lived your life and rewarded you a beautiful place in His kingdom. Why would you want to leave?

If God did not find favor with you and punished you with a not-so-desirable place in His kingdom, it would stand to reason that you would want to move on and hope for a better new life. And that again is the love of God. He wants them to have another chance to live a good and God-fearing life. Also, remember that you are allowed to take some of the knowledge that you have gained here with you into your next life.

As a newborn baby, all this knowledge will be very clear to you. But as you grow older, this knowledge will start to fade. As this knowledge fades, it will be your place to reject evil, greed, and lust. For your whole life, deep inside you, you will know what is right and wrong. But sadly, the wrong or evil way may be more glamorous, more appealing and profitable than doing the right thing. You will walk beside God or walk away from Him.

This is where having parents that walk in the way of the Lord become very important in your life. When you are born, as a baby, you remember all of God's teachings. You are without sin, and you are pure in God's eyes. Having God-fearing parents, they will help you refuel your faith in God and His teachings.

A few times, when I went for a walk in the meadow by myself, out of curiosity, I would walk far out to the west. The peacefulness and beauty of these meadows make you want to stay forever. But the further I ventured west, there would be a strange feeling that would start to grow inside me. It was not a bad feeling; it was a feeling of great peace, love, and a feeling of being loved, a feeling that I have felt before. But I could not quite recognize it.

I am not a professional writer, so I will add this at this time. I am writing these notes from my dream that I had in the year 1996. This is the year 2023. I remember almost 100 percent of this dream and have been wanting to write these notes for several years. Some of these notes are my thoughts of this dream. I am not saying that God spoke to me, and I am not a messenger from God, but I also want to say that I truly believe in God, Jesus, and the Holy Ghost—the triune God. But again, I feel an obligation to share my dream.

This was a dream, and dreams jump from one place to another and sometimes repeat themselves as did this one. There are several things in this dream that I would like to preach to everyone. God made this world very perfect and so very simple. He made man and a woman (simple). He gave them all the food and water they needed. There was no hate or greed. The kingdom I describe in my dream is the type of place that He gave to Adam and Eve. (They too fell to the temptation of the devil.)

In God's kingdom, everything is beautiful and very simple with beautiful colors, along with gentle breezes. In our man-made kingdoms, there are huge castles to show off their wealth; gold, diamonds, and statues to adorn themselves. Another part of man's kingdom is to have power over other people, to be in control of them. Man will sacrifice the lives of their fellow men for their own greed. Power is a very large and evil type of greed. Inserting power and control over your fellow man is one of the worst sins that you can commit. Power is the most used sin this earth has ever had.

God made man to be strong and wise, then He made a woman to be his partner, the love of his life. Man is to protect and care for her. He is not to rule over her but to rule with her and hold her close. They will work as one and be faithful to one another (my thoughts).

This part of my dream, I had almost forgotten.

On one occasion, my sister and son came to me with a circumstance that I had, that I needed to address. I had a very close loved one that I had left behind. They were having a very hard time dealing with my death. God sometimes allows you to go back to their loved ones (in spirit) and give them comfort and to let them know that things are okay.

To go from God's kingdom back to the living, you enter this grand building going east. You walk into the darkness until you see the light of the living world. You give them spiritual signs to let them know that you are with them, and your love will always be with them. (Love is something that never dies.)

In spirit, you stay with your loved ones until they have found their way. (Time has a way of healing your heart; this is a gift from God: time to heal.) You are instructed that sometimes it is hard to leave them again. (You cannot stay.) Your body has already been given back to Mother Earth. Your soul has a new home in God's kingdom.

In this dream, my sister and son were the only two people I knew. When I went to the dark end of the walk, I thought maybe there were a few people I knew. I did not go to the right end of the walk, so there may have been someone I knew.

There was one lesson I learned from the dark side. The body and soul are two different entities. Your soul knows what is good and righteous. The soul knows love, kindness, forgiveness, and all the ways of the Lord. The body has worldly needs. It needs water, food, warmth from the cold to be cool from the heat. The body knows things like lust, greed, power, the need to have more than the next person. The more the body has, the more it wants. This also breeds overindulgence and glut. Most of this is normal, but this is when the body and soul must be in balance with each other. (This is when keeping company with evil people comes into play.) It is easier to do wrong when you are with people that are not followers of God.)

Success in life is when the body and soul work together and live in the ways of the Lord. Your soul knows that the body needs worldly things, and that is good. The soul has the true answer to every problem (or question you may have). The body knows what is right or wrong. But sometimes, the wrong way looks more appealing.

But again, you can become very successful in life and be living in the ways of the Lord. God does reward those that follow in His path. But again, you must realize where your great success comes from. This will be one of the many tests of your faith. (A very successful man will share their success with others, which is very favorable in eyes of the Lord.)

Too much money and power are the devil's most effective tools to steal your soul. When it comes to money and power, the body is totally weak. This is where that soul must take control. This is also when going to church or a place of worship comes into play. A place of worship is where you refuel your faith in God. Remember that lots of money or lots of worldly things is not a successful life. Love of God, children, and happiness are things that make a successful life.

I want to go back to when I walked to the left. This journey was not a short one; it was very long. It was a journey of seeing and learning. In life, you can be told something, and you understand. But seeing something has a bigger impact on your understanding. God placed me in a very beautiful spot in His kingdom. From where I called home to the darkest place in His kingdom was a very far distance. The decline of the landscape and weather was a very slow process. I had already walked for some time, and the beauty of this place was still fantastic, and you would still be proud to be here. Their flowers and trees were not quite as wonderful as my place. The farther you journey left, the greater the decline in beauty. The sky goes from a beautiful blue to a gray sky with no sun. Then from gray to almost black and roars of thunder, the beautiful meadow turns to not-so-desirable weeds and barren soil. When you reach the darkest point in this journey, you see only sadness. The meadows have turned into a field of thorns. And without the beautiful sunlight, there is no light inside this beautiful building. Their souls are in total darkness. Yet God is still here to give them another chance for a better and spiritual life.

Even in this godforsaken place, God is still here with these poor souls. He has locked away evil and greed and all dealings with the devil, so they can see the ways of the Lord. Remember that memories of the lessons you have learned and memories of this place are taken into your next life. As a baby, you are without sin; you know the ways of the Lord. But as you grow, these memories start to fade. This point is when your body and soul must work together to live a good life. This is a lesson that is taught many times and is repeated many times while you are here. He wants you to take these lessons with you into your next life.

Is there a time when God gives up on these lost souls? This question was not answered or discussed in my dream. But with all that was in my dream, the answer would be that He never gives up on a lost soul.

These are my thoughts on when the body and soul part. When we die, the soul is sent to God to stand before God and be judged. The body is sent back to the earth to return to dust and making way for a new generation to inherit the earth.

When I was very young, I read a poem about a man who had died and was buried next to a large, white oak tree. The tree had consumed his body, and now he was part of the big oak tree. He lived again in this magnificent tree. I have thought about this all my life. So here are my thoughts about this: The average person today is put in a casket and then put into a vault. *Why?* You are never going to come back to life. Your body has very little value in terms of dollars. We belong to the earth, so you should return to the earth. The earth has given you everything you have needed your entire life. Your soul has already met with God to be judged.

These are my wishes. I want to be buried under a white oak tree. The tall oak tree will be my headstone. I want to be laid on a soft white sheet with pictures of my loved ones in my hands, dig me a deep hole, extralong and extrawide. I want some good black rich soil, put it about two feet deep. I want to be laid face up and then fill my grave with the same, black, rich soil. In time, the big, white oak will consume my body. I then will live in the branches of my magnificent headstone. I will give shelter to the red and blue birds, the orioles and robins. I will give them a place to build their nest and raise their young. I will watch the sun rise in the east and set in the west. I will feel and hear the gentle breeze as it passes through my leaves. On those stormy nights with strong winds, my magnificent headstone and I will stand strong and protect those that live within your branches. Your soul is what truly matters. It goes to God to be judged, so what better gift could you give yourself but to give your body back to Mother Earth.

My writings have drifted away from my dream, but my dream fills my head with other thoughts of life and the life after, my thoughts of the life I have lived. I have always thought of myself as a good man, thoughtful of others, kind and giving—in all, a very good person. Now I set in judgment of myself (not so good). I weed out all the good things I have done and focus on the evil and wrong things I have done. The bad outweighs the good. I have hurt people; I have broken promises, and I have lied. After judging myself and my life, I am ashamed. I can only hope that there is some truth in my dream.

All the lessons learned while in God's kingdom are written in the Bible. But words on a piece of paper can be misinterpreted, and even words changed to alter the lessons. Man has created words, like *close enough, good enough, maybe, next time,* and *will later.* Some of these words diminish the true teaching of God.

I am going to jump to another subject at this point.

I don't remember learning anything about this subject in my dream. But it has been a question in my mind for several years.

God made this world the way He wanted it. He has let the world evolve through time. For example, He made all different trees. The walnut tree does not cross with an oak tree. A pine tree does not cross with an apple tree. But now the apple tree can cross with some different types of fruit trees. And the oak tree can cross with different types of oak trees. We cannot deny evolution, but God created evolution. Many things have changed from when He first created the earth.

This same thing is true with plants and animals. This goes on into humans. A human can cross with a gorilla and an ape. But this would be immoral and totally wrong. But it can happen. Where does God put His limits on the subject? I think that your science and research is going too far with some of these things. I will drop this subject because I have no answers. God will address this subject in time.

I am back with things I learned from this dream.

On one occasion I was with a large group of people. We were all sitting under a large oak tree, and we were having a lone conversation about life on earth. The subject of large churches and wealthy priests came up. There was one man who took charge of this subject.

A church or a temple is a place to give thanks and worship God, a place to renew your knowledge of the ways of the Lord. It should be a place to refuel your faith in God.

This does not pertain to all churches and their congregation. But some churches have lost their way on this subject. Some churches have become a place to come and just socialize and show their wealth. For some priests, this has become a profession and not a calling. God will reward a priest who has a true heart. But a very wealthy priest is only stealing from God. If you give $100 a week to your priest, and he puts it in his pocket, have you helped save a lost soul? Have you fed a hungry person? No, you just made your priest wealthier.

A poor man that can't even feed is family may not be able to even go to this church. He may even be looked down on by the rest of the congregation. But if you take your $100 and buy this man and his family food and drink and tell him that it is a gift from God, you just may be able to save this soul.

Giving to God does not mean that you should give to a large and wealthy church. If God is not in that church, then it is not a church. A true church or place of worship can be anywhere where God is. It can be in your home, in your car, your place of work, or in the middle of a field if God is present in your heart. Giving does not always mean giving money. You can give food, kindness, forgiveness, encouragement, and even a prayer. A helping hand is also looked upon as a gift from God. It is not hard to please God, and you will be rewarded in the end.

Can you imagine a priest that is worth ten million dollars and lives in a fifteen-million-dollar home and preaches in a fifty-million-dollar church? How much food and how many lives could be changed with that kind of money? And all that money belongs to God. How many souls could be saved? A hungry man that can't even feed his family sometimes losses hope and turns to evil ways.

Jesus walked the earth and preached God's word without pay. Jesus owned nothing, and He asked for nothing. But He gave His entire life serving His Father, and He gave His life. Many of these rich and wealthy priests preach about giving money but not about God.

But God wants you to go to a place of worship. He wants you to hear His words from a true priest that has made this his calling. He needs you to give what you can so His words can be taught to all that want to hear. Yes, a man that teaches God's word should be paid but not to the extent of being wealthy.

Let's talk about death. Death is not a bad thing. You have a body and a soul. Only the body dies; the soul lives forever. The body goes back to the earth, and the soul goes to God. No matter how young or old you are or if you are having a happy life or a sad life, if you are living a God-fearing life and you die, you will be going to a better place. The only thing about dying is that you are leaving loved ones behind, and they will miss you. Death is only sad for the living.

I remember, when I was young, I had a close friend. He was tall, good-looking, very athletic, and could do anything. He had more girlfriends than most men dream of. When he was in his early twenties, he was happily married with lots of good friends and a good job. Then one day, he had a massive stroke. It left him paralyzed on one side of his body for the rest of his life. He was paralyzed from head to toe. He did learn to talk and verily walked but never regained the use of his arm and hand. This eliminated his marriage, his job, and a lot of his friends.

One day, he and I met for lunch. He started talking about his life. (We were in our early fifties at the time.) To my total surprise, he started talking about God and the miserable life he had to live. He was not mad at God; that was another total surprise. In our conversation, he made the comment that he would be happy when he died. And I ask *why*. He told me that God had promised him that He would take him out of that miserable body and give him a new one. This left me without words.

I need to get back to my dream.

I don't know how long I have been here, but I have seen many faces come and go. There were some who have been here longer than I have, and I am sure that some were going to stay forever. While you are here, there are no strangers—even more reasons to stay. But your soul remembers your past life and the earthly body it had. Maybe in your next life, you could serve God in a better way. You are also granted some earthly pleasures that are favorably looked upon by God.

I especially enjoyed walking in the meadows and just listening to nature. On many occasions, I would walk farther to the west, and each time I would get that strange feeling. The farther I went, the stronger that feeling became. I was fascinated by going west and wanted to see what it was about as a new beginning. And the longer I stayed in the far-western meadows, the stronger these feelings became.

I don't know why, but it was time for me to start a new life. And I was ready to start. I knew I would be leaving my son and sister, but they both said that they too would be leaving in time. They both gave me their blessings on my decision.

Maybe God had more plans for me. I had learned so much while I was here.

The time for me to leave had come. My son and sister, Patsy, walked with me into the meadow. We stopped under our favorite oak tree to chat and say our goodbyes. Saying goodbye was not going to be easy. I was leaving some of the ones that I love and the ones that

I had reconnected with. Leaving a paradise like this and going into the unknown sounds crazy.

My journey begins with many fears and uncertainties.

As I go farther out in the meadow, I find where my father and mother had buried their old life's inventories. In hopes of being with my same parents again, I buried my life inventory nearby. As I continued my way, I heard my son calling out to me. As I turned, I could see him waving his arms and calling to me. "If it is okay with you, I would love to see you in a few years." This was the statement that I was longing to hear. This made my decision much easier, knowing that my son would be in my next life. I was waving my arms, calling out, "*Yes.*" God had granted me my wish. I started to run back to give him a hug and tell him how much I loved him, but that strange feeling started to get stronger; it started pulling me toward the future. It started to overcome the desire to go back. As it got stronger and stronger, I remember that feeling.

That feeling was happening now. It was the longing to be held in my mother's arms.

Remember, this was a dream. Seventy-five percent of my writing is from my dream; the rest are my thoughts—not all, but most of my dream can be found in the Bible.

I am going to add this to my story (dream). This was a small part of that dream, but it did not make any sense, so I left it out. It did not fit in with the rest of my dream. But again, it was there and had a purpose. So I will add this small piece into my story. I will title this part "Trust."

This part took place on my first trip to the left (south), not far from where I called home. I came across a very large garden. This garden did not have any fences or any type of barrier to keep people out. This garden was abundant with every type of fruit and vegetables. Everything was ripe and ready to be consumed.

In front of this garden was a small archway. You had to enter through this gateway to be able to harvest your goods. If you were a person with money, you had to stop and make a list of what you were going to get, and you had to pay for each item before you entered.

If you were poor and had no money, you had to stop and tell the attendant that you could not pay. The poor man would be told that he could enter and get only what he needed for free.

When you are done collecting your goods, you do not go back through the entrance, but you exit this garden at any exit you wish. You exit the garden with no accountability for what you are taking.

The man with money had to pay for the same goods that the poor man was getting for free. Was it okay for the man with money to take more than what he paid for? He was trusted to take only what he paid for; more than that would be stealing. But they were giving the poor man his goods for free.

We went to the poor man; he was told to take what he needed, and it would be free. Was it okay for the poor man to take more than he needed? It was all free, and the man with money paid for his, so what would it hurt to take a little extra? If he takes more than he needs, this is stealing.

God does not judge you, weather you are rich or poor, but the word *trust* has the same meaning for both.

The reason I did not put this in my first writings. Is that there is no money in God's kingdom, and there is no food nor is there a need for food.

This was one of God's lessens. Can you be trusted when no one is watching? *Trust* has many meanings. We must *believe* and *trust* in God.

The more I think about this, maybe this lesson was specifically meant for me.

This dream was twenty-seven years ago. There have been countless hours that I have had to run this through my brain. There have been sleepless nights and hours of quiet times that I have had to think about this.

Do I believe in this dream? Do I believe in all of it or maybe part of it? I do believe in the parts of it that are written in the Bible, but there is a lot of it that is not mentioned in the Bible. I do not want to believe that my son passed before me. Was I supposed to write this? (I do not know.) There are a few dreams that I remember parts of. This one has played through my brain a thousand times. Something or someone is telling me to write this.

My grandfather was a Lutheran minister. Maybe he came to kick my ass and tell me to get myself ready for what's coming.

Before I started writing, I looked up several words to make sure I had the true definition of each.

I looked up the word *paradise* in an old *Webster's Dictionary*: the garden of Eden; any place of happiness; heaven; the uppermost gallery in a theater.

In my dream, where I was placed, that was my vision of paradise. God painted this paradise for me. As I walked to the left, my vision of paradise faded very fast, to the point it became my vision of what I thought hell would look like.

God is in control of hell also. At some point, God completely takes away paradise. Even in hell, God is still in control, and still, He is with these souls. God has always been stronger than the devil. God turned the devil loss to tempt your soul. God lets the devil tempt us in many ways, but deep down, we all know what is right and what is wrong.

If I had walked to the right, what would paradise look like? Would it have had snowcapped mountains, with large waterfalls and crystal-clear streams flowing through a grassy meadow? Deer, elk, and bison were grazing in the tall grass while the majestic eagle kept watch from above. I understand people that live in different parts of the world would have different visions of paradise. I guess that paradise is in the eyes of the beholder.

Paradise does not have to be a place. It can be a mother having enough food to feed her children. It can be a weary soldier when the fighting stops, seeing a newborn grandchild for the first time, watching your child grow up to be a good person.

Paradise is a very large word. No matter what or where your paradise is, there is only one artist, one paintbrush, one God.

I wish everyone could have a dream like this one. Deep down, we all know what is right and what is wrong. We all act before we think. God gave us hearing. We know what to listen to and what not to. He gave us eyes, and we know what to look at and what not to look at. He gave us a speech, but so many times we said the wrong things. These are more of God's tests.

Don't get me wrong, I have not lived a perfect life after this dream. But I do think more before I do or say something. But I am like most people; the first words that come out of my mouth are fast and are the wrong things to say. And doing the wrong things sometimes are more exciting and rewarding but not in the eyes of God.

Having a dream like this one makes you think about what is important. It makes your heart a little bigger; your smile gets a little wider. It makes you talk more about doing the right things, helping people that are in need. You talk more and without hesitation about God and His wishes. It also helps you forget about the things that you do *not* have. Good memories are the most important things you need, and the more the better. God says that you can take them with you, and no one can take them from you.

There is part of this dream that I left out. I will not talk about it; it will go to my grave. During my time in this dream, twice my son was called to meet with God Himself. He told me what it was about. This was something between God and him.

Earlier I wrote about priest that have become very wealthy from their teachings of the Bible. They are keeping God's money for themselves. I question myself as to why I am writing this book. I do want people to read it. Am I any better than the people I criticize?

Back to the subject of memories, in my dream, I received an inventory of my life. In it, there were memories of my entire life. There were good and bad, sad and happy, and there were the dark memories, dark memories that you never wanted to relive or see again.

After closing that inventory of my life, all the bad memories disappeared, gone forever. God had erased all the bad one for me. From this point on, there are only good memories, giving us a new start. I do not know how this plays out for the souls that are placed to the far left. He has forgiven them of their bad doings, but the erasing of their bad memories—I don't know.

I looked up the word *dream* in the old *Webster's Dictionary*: a train of thoughts or images passing through the mind during sleep; an idle fancy; to see or imagine in sleep; think about vainly; to have a train of ideas in sleep.

I have had thousands of dreams in my life. Most of them I didn't remember the next day. Some of them were so real that I woke up still thinking they were real. Some were so bad that my heart was racing when I woke. I have had the same dreams several times.

One of those dreams was when two black bulls had me trapped in a barn. It was getting dark, and no one came looking for me. I had this dream several times, but in life this never happened.

Years ago, I had a dear friend that had passed away. For several years, she would come to me in my dreams. In one of my dreams, she told me about a loved one of mine that was going to be very sick, but they would get well. (This did come true.) She would be in many of my dreams, with a big smile and good news for me. One time, she came with a big smile and told me she came to straighten my ass out. I would always wake up with a smile and be happy to have seen her. She hasn't been in my dreams for many years, something I truly miss. She would be one of God's favorite souls.

This dream was totally different. At the time of this dream, I was not a very religious person. I did know God, and I did believe in God, but I did not take Him very seriously. When you are young, you sometimes put other priorities before God.

I know that a dream only lasts a few seconds, but this one was very precise and so detailed with color and clarity. And I still remember every detail, every word, and every lesson that it gave.

It made me think of what I could live without. When you take away all the things that we really don't need, it takes us back to the garden of Eden. We do not need to have more money than the next person. We do not need a bigger house or a newer car. I don't even need this computer that I am using to write this story.

This will be my last thought: Christianity.

Christians have been killed by the hundreds of thousands just because of our beliefs. This is still going on in the world today.

We remove Christmas trees and the cross from stores because it offends some other religions. We change the word Christmas to Xmas or the word holidays so we won't offend other people. If they could kill us all or wipe up Christianity, they would. It is time to stop this bullshit.

I think this is bullshit. The book of the Muslim religion (the Quran preaches violence against non-Muslim) teaches their children and their grandchildren to kill my children and my grandchildren because we are Christians. We need to start standing up for our beliefs, start standing up for our God. I think we should start protecting our beliefs. I don't think God wants us to let these nonbelievers to stop us from spreading His word. Christianity needs protecting at all costs. He sacrificed His Son for us, so it is time to give back to Him.

My stop along the way to paradise.

39

ABOUT THE AUTHOR

Taroka Gorge in Taiwan

He was born in rural Missouri to the best parents anyone could be blessed with. His father was born in 1909, part Irish and part German. He was a hardheaded but very loving man. In the early 1930s, he trained to be a prizefighter to help support his family. Later he became the boxing coach for the county boxing team then later was a full-time farmer—Lowell O'Neal.

His mother was born in 1911, full-blood German, born in Eagle River, Wisconsin. Her father was a Lutheran minister. After graduating high school, his mother went to Ann Arbor Michigan College (my grandfather's alma mater) and studied to be an English teacher. But that all changed when she met his dad. She would be a farmer's wife and raise fourteen children—Ruth Mueller O'Neal.

He was number twelve of fourteen kids. He grew up on a farm with a Christian faith and plenty of brothers and sisters to fight with and learn from (not all good). He had a very good childhood. he has been tied to agriculture since birth. He never even thought once about writing a book.

He raised two very smart and good-looking sons, who have done well in life. They too have raised smart and hardworking families, giving him six grandchildren and five great-grandchildren.

He has worked in Oklahoma oil fields construction in Kansas City. He worked at a steel company, where he was the manager for four years. Then he went on to government inspections, traveling from Wisconsin to Texas and from Kansas to Ohio.

But with all these different jobs, he still stayed living on his father's farm, raising mostly cattle. But farming was not his friend. He lost more money than he ever made, but it is the home that he loves.

He has had many dreams in his life, and they, for the most part, have been forgotten but for one dream in 1996; it stays 100 percent in his thoughts. This dream has changed his thoughts of life and has eliminated any fears of death. Death is not an ending; it is a beginning.

With a promise to his granddaughter that he would try his hand at writing, he sat down and started to write down his dream. At the age of seventy-two, he is starting a new chapter in his life and hoping to find one last sip of God's sweet summer wine, something he never dreamed of doing and didn't think he could (not saying he can, but he gave it a try).

His life has been very full. He has a beautiful family. He has children, grandchildren, and great-grandchildren. And he has a love of his life that he thanks God for every day. (She has a heart of gold and a smile to match.) I have been well off financially and have been broke many times, but he has never been without his faith. Faith does not care how much money he has.

Don't get it wrong, even though he believes in God and trusts and depends on Him, he has more than his share of sins to account for and many skeletons in his closet.

He has lived a very simple life with many regrets. But given the chance, he would not change one second of his life. Changing one part of your life could change your life completely.